Flowers

Ernestine Giesecke

Heinemann Library
Des Plaines, Illinois

©1999 Reed Educational & Professional Publishing
Published by Heinemann Library,
an imprint of Reed Educational & Professional Publishing,
1350 East Touhy Avenue, Suite 240 West
Des Plaines, IL 60018

Designed by Lindaanne Donohoe
Printed in Hong Kong

03 02 01 00 99
10 9 8 7 6 5 4 3 2 1

Library of Congress Cataloging-in-Publication Data

Giesecke, Ernestine, 1945–
    Flowers / Ernestine Giesecke.
        p.   cm. — (Outside my window)
    Includes bibliographical references (p.) and index.
    Summary: Presents brief introduction to the characteristics of
flowers and provides photographs and simple information to help the
reader identify such flowers as the dandelion, lily, and rose.
    ISBN 1-57572-683-1 (lib. bdg.)
    1. Flowers—Juvenile literature. 2. Plants—Juvenile literature.
[1. Flowers—Identification. 2. Plants—Identification.] I. Title.
II. Series: Giesecke, Ernestine, 1945– Outside my
window.
QK653.G54 1998
582.13—dc21

98-6359
CIP
AC

Acknowledgments

The publisher would like to thank the following for permission to reproduce copyright photographs:

Cover: First Image West, Inc./Tom Neiman

Tony Stone Images, Inc./Greg Vaughn, pp. 4, 12; Earth Scenes/Patti Murray, pp. 5 top, 9, 18;
First Image West, Inc./Tom Neiman, pp. 5 bottom, 10, 16, 20; Earth Scenes/Breck P. Kent, pp.6,
14, 15; Earth Scenes/E.R. Degginger, pp. 7 top, 7 middle; Oxford Scientific Film/Deni Brown, p. 8;
Oxford Scientific Film/Gil Bernard, p. 11 top; Tony Stone Images, Inc./Everett Johnson, p. 11 bottom;
Phil Martin, pp. 7 bottom, 13, 17 top and bottom, 19, 22, back cover; First Image West, Inc./
Robert Dawson, p. 21.

Every effort has been made to contact copyright holders of any material reproduced in this book.
Any omissions will be rectified in subsequent printings if notice is given to the publisher.

Some words are shown in bold, **like this.** You can find out what they mean by
looking in the glossary.

Contents

Outside Your Window

You can learn about nature by looking out your window. Look outside your window at home or school to see flowers. Flowers are part of nature.

Look closely and you will see that flowers are different from one another. No matter where you live, you should see most of the flowers in this book.

What is a Flower?

A flower is part of a plant. Flowers have a special job to do for plants. Flowers make the seeds that grow into new plants.

- pollen
- petal
- seed-making parts
- leaf
- stem

Flowers look different at different times. They are only seen when the plant is in bloom.

1. A flower first appears as a **bud.**

2. Then the flower opens and you can see its color.

3. When a flower grows old and dry, its seeds are ready to become new plants.

Clover

You can find clover in fields and grassy areas. Look closely. Clover creeps along the ground. The flowers are small.

Most clover **stems** have three leaves.
You'll be lucky if you find a clover with
four leaves. Bees and rabbits like clover.
Bees use the clover to make honey. Rabbits
eat the leaves and stem of the plant.

**MORE
ABOUT
CLOVER**

- Height:
  1½ inches
  (4 cm)
- Color:
  white
  or pink
- blooms
  from
  spring
  to fall

Dandelion

Dandelions can grow in the cracks of sidewalks. The edge of a dandelion leaf has tiny teeth. They look like a lion's teeth. That is how the dandelion got its name.

As the dandelion grows older, the bright yellow flowers turn into fluffy white seed heads. The seeds are carried by the wind to a new place to grow.

Sunflower

The sunflower stands straight and tall. The dark center of the sunflower is called the *disk*. Around the disk are yellow **rays.** Birds and squirrels eat sunflower seeds. People like to eat sunflower seeds, too.

Some sunflower seeds have two pointed teeth. The teeth help the seeds stick to animal fur and to clothes. This is how the seeds get carried to a new place to grow.

MORE ABOUT SUNFLOWERS

- Height: 2 to 10 feet (1 to 3 m)
- Color: yellow
- blooms from late summer to fall

Lily

The lily looks like a trumpet. **Lilies** have long and narrow leaves. The leaves start at the bottom of the plant.

Under the soil, the lily has a **bulb** and **roots.** Inside the bulb is food to last through the winter and to feed new flowers in spring. The onions you eat are in the same family as these lily flowers.

Rose

Be careful! A rose looks pretty and smells nice. But it has sharp, pointed thorns on its **stem.** The thorns protect the plant from animals that might eat it.

A wild rose has five petals around a yellow center. **Cultivated** roses have many, many more petals. Rose seeds are inside the fruit of the rose flower. The fruit is called the *rose hip.* Some people drink tea made from rose hips.

MORE ABOUT ROSES

- Height: 1 to 3 feet (30 cm to 1m)
- Color: many colors
- blooms from late spring to summer

17

Queen Anne's Lace

Queen Anne's Lace is a tall, thin plant. The flower is a flat circle of tiny white flowers. The leaves are frilly and lacy.

• Height:
  1 to 3 feet
  (30 cm to 1 m)

• Color:
  creamy
  white

• blooms
  from
  spring
  to fall

Under the soil, Queen Anne's Lace has a long **taproot.** The taproot looks like a carrot. That is why the plant is sometimes called wild carrot.

Cattail

MORE ABOUT CATTAILS

- Height: 3 to 9 feet (1 to 3 m)
- Color: brown
- blooms from spring to summer

Can you imagine a brown flower? Look for cattails along the edges of rivers, lakes, or ponds. The dark brown tail is make up of many tiny flowers. Long ago, people crushed cattail roots to make flour for baking.

Prickly Pear

The prickly pear is one of the few flowers that grows well in hot, dry places. Its red and yellow flowers are a bright sight in the desert. Prickly pears have sharp **spines** all around. The spines make it difficult for animals to eat the plant or its flower.

MORE ABOUT PRICKLY PEARS

- Height: up to 1 foot (30 cm)
- Color: yellow
- blooms from spring to summer

21

Flower Bookmarks

1. Place flowers between sheets of newspaper or paper towels. Cover with one or two books.

2. Cut a small piece of cardboard.

3. When the flowers are flat and dry, glue them to the cardboard.

4. Now you have the finished flower bookmark!

Glossary

bud	beginning of a flower
bulb	underground bud of a plant
cultivated	plants grown for sale
lilies	more than one lily
rays	yellow parts around the disk of a sunflower
roots	underground parts of a plant that collect water and food from soil
spines	long, sharp needles
stem	main part of a plant that holds flowers
taproot	large root from which smaller roots grow

More Books to Read

Cooper, Jason. *Flowers*. Vero Beach, Fla: Rourke Press, 1991.

Fowler, Allan. *What's Your Favorite Flower?* Danbury, Conn: Children's Press, 1993.

Mettler, Rene. *Flowers*. New York: Scholastic, Inc., 1993.

Flowers in This Book

Index